DR. R

MW01287309

PREACHING JUDE

PREPARING EXPOSITORY HOLINESS
SERMONS ON ONE OF THE NEW TESTAMENT'S
MOST POWERFUL LETTERS

dustjacket

Published by Dust Jacket Press
Preaching Jude: Preparing Expository Holiness Sermon's on One of the New Testament's Most Powerful Letters / Rudy Morgan

ISBN: 978-1-947671-81-2

Dust Jacket Press
P. O. Box 721243
Oklahoma City, OK 73172
www.dustjacket.com

Cover and interior design: D. E. West / ZAQ Designs & Dust Jacket Creative Services

Printed in the United States of America

www.dustjacket.com

CONTENTS

Acts 18:24–26 gives us the beautiful story of the exemplary leadership couple Priscilla and Aquila. This couple was instrumental in helping a phenomenally gifted young leader, Apollo, in having a better grasp of the faith he had come to embrace and of its message he had felt called to proclaim. Priscilla and Aquila's action reflect definitely what has been the passion and sense of mission of author Rudy Morgan. From my earliest memory of him when we were young adults together, he has always been motivated and engaged like Priscilla and Aquila to help us all get a better grasp on our common faith.

In the present work Morgan draws on the disciplines of biblical theology, biblical interpretation, and the principles of expository preaching. Dr. Morgan in his own long experience as a minister makes available to all, but in particular to beginning preaching practitioners, insights that will inevitably give them a better understanding of the faith and more importantly of the preaching task. This book, like others such as *A Little Exercise for Young Theologians,* by Helmut Thielke, is a valuable resource in the process of ministerial formation.

This work reflects the author's deep Wesleyan roots. Albert C. Outler identies "the Wesleyan quadrilateral" as Scripture, tradition, reason, and experience. Morgan indicates in these pages his absolute confidence in Scripture as the final authority and absolute basis for faith and practice. He also demonstrates the importance of a thorough knowledge of relevant church history and its benefit in the interpretive task.

As a true Wesleyan, the author is not afraid to make scholarly inquiry; this is evident in the references used in the academic warrants for his conclusions. Finally, as with all true Wesleyans, Morgan finds that experience is valid and very important. Therefore, he confidently refers to and draws upon his personal experience as a preacher to illustrate and elucidate vital points that he seeks to cause the reader to understand.

Readers, beware! This work set out not only to inform but also to challenge and change people in their thinking and practice. It is expected that the following pages will therefore be challenged by the engaged reader. This is not intended to be relaxing reading. The expectation is for the reader to wrestle with this material so that as in the message seen in the first four verses in the ancient letter to Christians from Jude, the reader will become a "champion fighter" for the faith—because it is indeed worth fighting for.

—Dr. Samuel Vassel
District Superintendent
Metro New York District
Church of the Nazarene

PREFACE

This book is an attempt to encourage expository Holiness preaching further. Quality preaching if done faithfully is hard work but gives great reward each time for the preacher who ministers regularly and lovingly and to the congregation who receives the Word. So as not to be scatterbrained in sharing, I have decided to use my favorite Bible book of one chapter, Jude, as the basis and center for this searching and encouraging book.

This book is intended to be read slowly, critically, with reflection and prayer. It is merely reaffirming that the most important biblical principle for expository preaching is found in 2 Timothy 3:16–17: "All Scripture is God-breathed and is useful for teaching, rebuking, correcting and training in righteousness, so that the servant of God may be thoroughly equipped for every good work."

You will find contained in the pages of this book one solid example of how detailed and involved the preparation of an expository message or any other type of sermon should be. It also expands the density and diversity reflected in sharing an address under the anointing of the Holy Spirit. Each person/ preacher who reads can take the principles shared and apply to the background, resources, and personality of the one God designed and called.

One reason for this book is to voice a preference for expository Holiness preaching, which has dominated many seasons. In the twenty-first century expository Holiness preaching must become stronger, not weaker, and practiced regularly. The content of this book is only one example of a framework or structure that could be used to develop definite expository Holiness sermons. I have been preaching now for over forty-five years, and I'm still learning. I desire to pass along a little of what God has allowed me to receive. I have learned from good and bad in others and found the lessons to be helpful.

This short book is first written for fellow preachers (especially younger ones) and also laypeople who love the Lord very much and are called to feed the Word well to people they serve. I hope readers of this book will be challenged to pray more faithfully for their preachers to become better and proficient. Preachers like us always need your constructive encouragement and feedback to become improved at the craft.

Hopefully someone will read this book and God will call him or her for the first time to preach the Word. To be called by God to teach and preach is a holy and joyful responsibility that requires diligence and total commitment to the leading of the Holy Spirit. How does God call someone to preach or to some other area of specialized ministry? Has God been calling you to teach and preach? There are three distinct divine ways I will briefly mention.

1. God speaks to you directly (like God calling Moses to serve—Exodus 3:1–12).

2. God speaks to you indirectly (as in God communicating to you through the preached Word of someone else, reading a book, and so on).

3. God speaks to you as you obediently follow Jesus in the circumstances you face in the journey of life. You follow closely God's glaring "green lights" and "red lights" in your daily living.

"The realization of the call in a person's life may come like a clap of thunder, or it may dawn gradually. But however quickly or slowly this awareness comes, it is always accompanied by an undercurrent of the supernatural—something that is inexpressible and produces a 'glow'" (Oswald Chambers, *My Utmost for His Highest,* September 29 devotional).

The Lord called me to preach through the third way mentioned above. I will praise God until I die for the highest honor of proclaiming the Word of God. When God calls someone to preach or to accomplish any mission for Him, the problem that interferes is always the obedience of the person's will. Is your will given completely to your Savior and have you been entirely filled with the Holy Spirit? *When God calls you, leave everything and follow Jesus* (reflect on the importance of full surrender to Christ by remembering His call to the first disciples in Luke 5:1–11). Your obedience will bring the greatest fulfillment in your life as you diligently trust and obey the Lord. The goal and paramount desire of all disciples of Christ are to genuinely do the will of the Lord.

And now I strongly urge you *not* to do what the young man in the Bible did: "Jesus . . . said to him, 'You still lack one thing. Sell everything you have . . . then come, follow me.' When he heard this, he became very sad, because he was very wealthy" (Luke 18:22–23). The call of Jesus may sound harsh or unyielding initially but He will not back down or water down the command from heaven. The young man walked away sorrowfully and discouraged because he understood the profound depth of the hand of God on his life and was saying no. Jesus calls us not to "freeze" us but to give us the freedom to be the best we can be. Have you been struggling with that call from God? One unique aspect of the grace of God is that He will never throw your past sins and disobedience in your face when you finally say yes.

As you reflect you may be saying, "Jesus doesn't understand all I'll need to give up and the lives of others who will be affected." Yes, Jesus knows all that and also the perils of the unknown future that is ahead for you following Jesus in the pulpit and possibly pastoral ministry. Your unyielding commitment to holy living must be like that of the apostle Paul and all the other saints of God of the past and present—the commitment that in life or death you will go wherever He leads (see Philippians 1:21). Go and preach in obedience to Jesus and don't worry about the human needs of the body (see Luke 12:22). Count the cost, but don't fret when in the hands of Jesus (Psalm 37:1–8).

Therefore, I reiterate that your willingness to follow Jesus will bring the highest fulfillment to your life as you diligently and loyally follow Him every day of your life. Follow Him willingly in His gentle nudges and don't allow a God-ordained crisis to bring a drastic awakening. Your internal sacrifice and yielding of your whole will empower you through the Holy Spirit to follow only Jesus Christ, our Lord. This God-given joy is for the preacher and all other surrendered disciples. In supporting the call of God on your life, keep the focus on the loving nature and holiness of Him who calls you.

With all love to my brothers and sisters who have already started the grand journey of preaching, it is good to have seasons in which we worship God by reminding ourselves about the great privilege God has given in living and proclaiming the Word of God.

All the servants in the Bible would agree with the writing of the apostle Paul to all disciples of Christ today: "For the grace of God has appeared that offers salvation to all people. It teaches us to say 'No' to ungodliness and worldly passions, and to live self-controlled, upright and godly lives in this present age" (Titus 2:11–12).

ACKNOWLEDGMENTS

1. The late Rev. Farrell Chapman was a distinguished district superintendent of the Trinidad and Tobago District of the Church of the Nazarene. He was an enjoyable and fruitful servant of Christ and the Church of the Nazarene. He happened to be my first homiletics professor at Caribbean Nazarene College, Trinidad, West Indies. I am indebted to him for the many truths shared with me and others in that course. One of the things I took seriously was the advice that for the first several years of preaching I should write out a manuscript of each sermon. I appreciate to this day that Rev. Chapman allowed me to first serve in 1977 as a student preacher/pastor at Dow Village Church of the Nazarene, Trinidad, West Indies.

2. The late Rev. Noel O. Williams was a district superintendent of the Jamaica District of the Church of the Nazarene and earlier a superintendent in the Jamaica Wesleyan Holiness denomination. In the early days of learning to be a disciple of Christ, I had the highest privilege to sit under some of the most exceptional Holiness preaching as he declared the Word of God as my pastor at Richmond

Park Church of the Nazarene in Kingston, Jamaica. He was a giant of a servant in the pulpit, life itself, street preaching, and speaking before college students. One of the truths imprinted on me by Rev. Williams was that the Holiness message is not complete until I know how to share a pointed and meaningful altar call.

3. Rev. Aaron Blache has been a loving mentor for over forty years. He is now officially retired as a distinguished pastor in the Church of the Nazarene and is a former district superintendent of the Trinidad and Tobago District of the Church of the Nazarene. He is one of the finest exponents of Holiness preaching who can be found even to this day. I thank him for the privilege I had sitting under divine instruction at the Santa Cruz Church of the Nazarene in Trinidad and Tobago and at numerous revival services. That communication has continued for years and involved many fruitful occasions covering diverse subjects.

4. Dr. Roger L. Hahn has been a distinguished professor and Christian example for many years to countless people at Nazarene Theological Seminary, Kansas City. I still remember the privilege of taking a class on biblical hermeneutics under Dr. Hahn that had a lasting impact on me regarding the importance of preparing thoroughly to preach Holiness sermons and as such declaring the Word of God as effectively as possible.

5. The writer is very grateful to all scholars who work meticulously and continuously at accurately transcribing God's revelation in the Holy Bible.

6. Last, thank you to Jonathan Wright for his loving, meticulous, and excellent editing of this project. His thoughtful partnership is much appreciated. Also, the whole team at Dust Jacket Press, led by Adam Toler, is second to none as a Christian business enterprise.

INTRODUCTION

- Basic Thoughts for Preachers to Ponder
- The Book of Jude
- What Are Useful Definitions of Expository Preaching?
- What Is the General Composition of the Book of Jude?

Basic Thoughts for Preachers to Ponder

An excellent and maturing expository preacher (or any other worth his or her salt) reads extensively and grows to accumulate information and illustrations through his or her life. As a presenter of the good news of the gospel, you should continue developing your library and your background notes, sketches, and useful contemporary information in diverse formats. You should also be observant of the news in the world while you feed your soul on the Word each day.

Many years ago a preacher told me correctly in Jamaican colloquial language, "God calls fools, but He does not keep any." That is also true for the orators of God's Word whom He calls to proclaim and prophesy before people. I have gloriously seen God turn people with a minimum academic background into persuasive and influential disciples sharing God's Word.

Now let's get down to working hard in a growing appreciation for the high value of preaching expository sermons. When we hunger to be filled and to learn, God supplies abundantly and teaches well at the depth we can receive.

Before you begin your preparation, remember to initiate any search with a heartfelt prayer to God about opening up truths for your mind and soul. Ask God to guide you as to what passage or text to preach on each occasion. *The Word and God's sheep belong to Him, and He knows how to best connect these two through you.*

Above all, live faithfully the truths of the Word that you share with other people. You will do this only if the Holy Spirit fills the totality of your life, and that includes your home life, conversations with friends, walking or driving, watching television, working at a computer, sleeping, and the simple facets of eating and drinking done all for the glory of God. Jesus must daily be the central person of your life and all you do. Live in maturing faith in Jesus until nothing He does with you each day surprises you.

The Book of Jude

Salutation

[1] Jude, a servant of Jesus Christ and brother of James,
To those who are called, who are beloved in God the Father and kept safe for Jesus Christ:
[2] May mercy, peace, and love be yours in abundance.

The Occasion of the Letter

³ Beloved, while eagerly preparing to write to you about the salvation we share, I find it necessary to write and appeal to you to contend for the faith that was once for all entrusted to the saints. ⁴ For certain intruders have stolen in among you, people who long ago were designated for this condemnation as ungodly, who pervert the grace of our God into licentiousness and deny our only Master and Lord, Jesus Christ.

Judgment on False Teachers

⁵ Now I desire to remind you, though you are fully informed, that the Lord, who once for all saved a people out of the land of Egypt, afterward destroyed those who did not believe. ⁶ And the angels who did not keep their own position, but left their proper dwelling, he has kept [held or remained is the writer's emphasis] in eternal chains in deepest darkness for the judgment of the great day. ⁷ Likewise, Sodom and Gomorrah and the surrounding cities, which, in the same manner as they, indulged in sexual immorality and pursued unnatural lust, serve as an example by undergoing a punishment of eternal fire.

⁸ Yet in the same way these dreamers also defile the flesh, reject authority, and slander the glorious ones. ⁹ But when the archangel Michael contended with the devil and disputed about the body of Moses, he did not dare

to bring a condemnation of slander against him, but said, "The Lord rebuke you!" 10 But these people slander whatever they do not understand, and they are destroyed by those things that, like irrational animals, they know by instinct. 11 Woe to them! For they go the way of Cain, and abandon themselves to Balaam's error for the sake of gain, and perish in Korah's rebellion. 12 These are blemishes on your love-feasts, while they feast with you without fear, feeding themselves. They are waterless clouds carried along by the winds; autumn trees without fruit, twice dead, uprooted; 13 wild waves of the sea, casting up the foam of their own shame; wandering stars, for whom the deepest darkness has been reserved forever.

14 It was also about these that Enoch, in the seventh generation from Adam, prophesied, saying, "See, the Lord is coming with ten thousands of his holy ones, 15 to execute judgment on all, and to convict everyone of all the deeds of ungodliness that they have committed in such an ungodly way, and of all the harsh things that ungodly sinners have spoken against him." 16 These are grumblers and malcontents; they indulge their own lusts; they are bombastic in speech, flattering people to their own advantage.

Warnings and Exhortations

17 But you, beloved, must remember the predictions of the apostles of our Lord Jesus Christ; 18 for they said to you,

"In the last time there will be scoffers, indulging their own ungodly lusts." [19] It is these worldly people, devoid of the Spirit, who are causing divisions. [20] But you, beloved, build yourselves up on your most holy faith; pray in the Holy Spirit; [21] keep yourselves in the love of God; look forward to the mercy of our Lord Jesus Christ that leads to eternal life. [22] And have mercy on some who are wavering; [23] save others by snatching them out of the fire; and have mercy on still others with fear, hating even the tunic defiled by their bodies.

Benediction

[24] Now to him who is able to keep you from falling, and to make you stand without blemish in the presence of his glory with rejoicing, [25] to the only God our Savior, through Jesus Christ our Lord, be glory, majesty, power, and authority, before all time and now and forever. Amen.

What Are Useful Definitions of Expository Preaching?

Expository preaching is one way of presenting the Word of God in which the preacher has carefully searched for the closest meaning of a particular text or passage of Scripture. To proclaim the Word in this way is to declare that the Bible means what it says unapologetically and needs to be heard by everyone. Exegesis (the first focus of this book) is the opening-up of professional and grammatical exposition or a careful drawing-out of the exact meaning of a passage in its original context.

Fruitful expository preaching then applies the searched journey of material gathered to spiritual, social, and moral applications that are important today for the lives of hearers (the second focus of this book).

Another way to state the meaning of expository preaching or detailed presentations is, first, the exposing of the original text or particular passage. The preacher then applies or gives purpose to the presentation gathered to the times and situations in which we live so hearers can have revealed light and be moved positively and assuredly by the Holy Spirit.

I strongly suggest that as we come closer to understanding the meaning of the words and context and grammar of a passage, we can better communicate God's inspired intrinsic value and applications to today's world. We will now begin the search for the original meaning of Jude without losing the primary focus on verses 1–4 as our main text exposed in this treatise.

What Is the General Composition of the Book of Jude?

The New Testament book of Jude may be divided into five sections, as seen from the bold headings in the text quoted earlier. Having read through the book numerous times (when preparing to preach—the contextual background essentials are necessary to pinpoint), I am convinced that there are three major sections:

A. Verses 1–4: Introduction and Purpose

B. Verses 5–19: Identification of the Enemies of the Church of Christ

C. Verses 20–25: Appropriate Response by the Church; Conclusion (Doxology)

For this book I will use the first four verses as the text for the building of three practical expository sermons (illustrated mostly in manuscript form) done later in this work. But to build an expository sermon I must understand well what the whole chapter is fundamentally saying.

Please note that verses 1–4 can be broken down into two main paragraphs. That is,

Verses 1–2: Prescript or Introduction

Verses 3–4: "Contend for the faith"—why?

Some translations of the Bible (always be wise and use more than one interpretation and paraphrase of the Bible when preparing a sermon) would readily support the paragraphs above as the literary units for verses 1–4. The book of Jude is referred to as being part of "the general epistles" of the New Testament. Jude is indeed a letter to Christian congregations in the first century and is named after its author, Jude. According to scholars, this name was quite common in biblical times and is a form of *Judas* and *Judah*. We will delve into this consideration later.

However, in *A Structural Commentary* (use all complementary resources available, and that includes print and the many reputable and multiple available Internet resources), the writer says about the book of Jude,

> *Internally, the epistle in verse 1 points to an author who is a "submitted person" in the definition of "doulos," the Greek word for "slave."... Thus, the author's "lived world" is organized by his submission to his faith system, which is early Messianic Christianity. This organized lived world points Jude in the direction of being dependent upon the care and love of God, having a stable, ethical standard of right vs. wrong, good vs. evil, and having a strong vision about the future. Thus, the classical hermeneutic [interpretation] posits Jude as a devout man who loved God and who hated evil, and who had faith that God was in control of world history.*[1]

It is difficult to find, and therefore I have little evidence about, the proposed author's spiritual and emotional development. However, we are confident that he was Jewish, for his writings show a productive "comfort level" with the Old Testament Scriptures [it is so important to reread thoroughly and thoughtfully the context of the Bible passage we are preaching from].

> *Jude sharply challenges one of them. . . . Greek ideals of "freedom" by calling himself a "slave" in the opening paragraph. . . . From this angle we can see Jude as a "radical" person within Greek and Hebrew society [any focused reading of Jude tells us that he was addicted to Jesus]; in other words, someone who has taken a stand against the normal mode of existence. Thus, we see Jude as a social radical who rejects the Greek ideal of freedom in favor of submitting himself as a voluntary slave to his Lord and Savior Jesus Christ.*[2]

Students of the Word classify the letter of Jude as a well-written "early catholic" document, meaning it was well circulated among the universal church groups of that period. The return of the Lord and the *parousia* hope is quite distinct in its message. As such, the letter (written in literary Greek) is better understood as early "apocalyptic Jewish Christian."

The *New Interpreter's Bible* states,

> *As the use of Jewish sources, apocalyptic texts, and tradition . . . indicates, Jude was working within the confines of Jewish Christianity, which had a vibrant apocalyptic outlook, and this outlook underlines his rhetorical approach. The letter is predominantly deliberate rhetoric, which by proofs and advice tries to persuade the audience to embrace*

what is advantageous, necessary, and expedient and dissuade from the opposite. The letter specifies that it aims to persuade the church "to contend for the faith" (v. 3)—that is, not to heed the false teacher's message and practice and thus come under same judgment at the encroaching Parousia. In its effort to persuade the church, the letter also relies upon epideictic rhetoric, which both praises and blames. Such rhetoric aims to uplift what is honorable and to cast down what is dishonorable, especially to increasing audience assent to honorable values.[3]

SECTION ONE

In this search for the original meaning of our text, we now gather information that addresses the following:

- The Important Message of the Book of Jude

- The Original Version of Jude

- The Historical Data Surrounding Jude

- When Was Jude Written?

- The Reason for the Letter of Jude

The Important Message of the Book of Jude

One particularly noteworthy feature seen in Jude is the appearance of triplets that amplify the message communicated in this book (verses 1–2, 5–7, 8, 11, 19, 20–21, 22–23, 25). For example, three types of ungodly persons are described, who find counterparts in the false teachers (verses 5–7); and the application of these descriptions to the false teachers is a triplet (verse 8). Also, words are cho-

sen for their associated imagery. Noteworthy is the image of prophecy and the interpretation of verses 11–13, which provide a strong negative characterization of the false teachers.[4]

The most important message taken from this letter, I believe, is found in verses 20–23, and not the Midrash (verses 5–19) or the application of historical writings to the contemporary situation of the time of Jude. Note that "the past tenses (verses 5–6, 9), prophetic aorists (verses 11, 14—an unqualified past tense of a verb), and future tenses (verse 18) of the citations, representing historical types and prophecies, are matched by present tenses in all the interpretations where Jude explains the fulfillment of the prophecies in the present."[5]

The letter of Jude seems carefully written, and its language is vivid and militant, demanding attention from the reader. The previous truth is a significant point to remember in preparing the actual sermon and presenting truths to the public. The first four verses of Jude only introduce the more important messages that follow.

The Original Version of Jude

As with the other books of the Canon, we do not have the original text for the letter of Jude, but on the subject of "sources" Bauckham writes,

Despite his competence in Greek, the author's real intellectual background is Palestinian Judaism. The assumption is that Jude, like many NT authors, habitually used the OT in its Greek version, the LXX [sometimes called the Greek Old Testament], but the assumption is mistaken. Of course, Jude shows he is familiar with the usual Greek renderings of certain OT Hebrew expressions; used both in the LXX and in later Jewish Greek literature. . . . Much more significant is the fact that at no point where he alludes to specific verses of the OT does he echo the language of the LXX. In two of these cases he must depend on the Hebrew text because the Septuagint does not give even the meaning he adopts (verse 12: Proverbs 25:14; verse 13: Isaiah 57:20). . . . This evidence shows that it was the Hebrew Bible with which Jude was familiar.[6]

The Historical Data Surrounding Jude

Remember that the writer we are looking at is Jude. The question, therefore, is this: Which one of the Judes (Judases) referred to in the New Testament is the actual author? William Barclay's discussion on the authorship of Jude proves quite helpful at this point. He writes,

In the New Testament there are five people called Judas.

A. *There is the Judas of Damascus in whose house Paul was praying after his conversion on the Damascus road (Acts 9:11).*

B. *There is Judas Barsabas, a leading figure in the councils of the Church, who, along with Silas, was the bearer to Antioch of the decision of the Council of Jerusalem. . . . This Judas was also a prophet (Acts 15:32).*

C. *There is Judas Iscariot.*

   None of these three [above] has ever been considered seriously as the author of this letter.

D. *There is the second Judas in the apostolic band. John calls him Judas, not Iscariot (John 14:22). In Luke's list of the Twelve, there is an apostle whom the Authorized Version calls Judas the brother of James (Luke 6:16; Acts 1:13). If we were to depend solely on the Authorized Version we might well think that here we have a serious candidate for the authorship of this letter, and indeed, the Church father Tertullian [prolific early Christian writer from roughly 155 to 240 AD) calls the writer "the Apostle Judas." But in the Greek this man is called merely "Judas of James." This is a very common idiom in Greek, and almost always it means not brother of but son of—so that*

Judas of James in the list of the Twelve is not Judas the brother of James but Judas the son of James, as all the more modern translations show.

E. *There is the Judas who was the brother of Jesus (Matthew 13:55; Mark 6:3). If any of the Judases of the New Testament is the writer of this letter, it must be this one, for only he could truly be called the brother of James [who was also one of the brothers of Jesus; the writings of Rose and Gutherie further support this writer].*

What are the objections to believing that Judas or Jude, the brother of Jesus, was the writer of this letter?

A. *If Jude . . . was the brother of Jesus, why does he not say so?*

B. *If the Jude of Palestine, who was the brother of Jesus, he could not have written the Greek of this letter, for it would be Aramaic that he spoke and not Greek. That is not a safe argument.*

C. *It might be that the heresy Jude is attacking is gnosticism and that gnosticism is much more a Greek way of thought that it is a Jewish way of thinking—and what would Jude of Palestine be doing writing to Greeks?*

D. *Last, if this letter had been known to have been the work of Jude or Judas the brother of Jesus, it would not have taken so long in gaining entry into the New Testament.*[7]

All the previous five objections fall "flat" when one interacts with them. Some scholars even suggest that the letter is pseudonymous (written by someone else using the name Jude).

None of these seem as meaningful and correct as the belief that Jude, the brother of Jesus, and James (first leader of the home church in Jerusalem) wrote our text contained in the letter of Jude.

When Was Jude Written?

Some scholars seem to suggest that the letter of Jude was written circa 50–80 AD. I find noteworthy what the *World Bible Commentary* says on the subject:

> *The opponents confronted in the letter are not second century Gnostics. Jude belongs to the milieu of Apocalyptic Jewish Christianity and combats the teacher's antinomian libertinism* [someone devoid of most moral and sexual restraints—too many persons, I note, are like that today in the USA].
> *. . . These features make it unlikely that the letter could be later than the end of the first century. . . . All the same, once one has cast off the spell of the*

early Catholic and AntiGnostic reading of Jude, the letter does give a general impression of primitiveness. Its character is such that dating in the '50s [is okay]*, and nothing requires a later date.*[8]

One accepts that the book of Jude is written to a church or unknown churches, but I feel that it was for churches in Asia Minor. (However, some scholars have suggested churches in Palestine, Syria, or Egypt. Needless to say, the church grew steadily and rapidly after the Pentecostal experience in Jerusalem). Our passage, as with the entire book, was written to Jewish Christians who are surrounded by Gentiles. It is important to note that the readers of Jude must have understood his numerous Old Testament illustrations.

Therefore, in the light of all the assembled information, I lean toward a later time for the writing of Jude, roughly 80–100 AD. But a big question mark remains. Some tradition claims that Jude suffered martyrdom about 65 AD in today's Beirut. If this is so, the letter had to be written before this date—meaning that I am still not sure of the actual time.

When doing honest research and the researcher is with doubt, he or she should not preach as truths what he or she is not sure of.

The Reason for the Letter of Jude

As we continue to examine the history of the passage we need to keep in mind the following:

The occasion of the letter is the infiltration of the church by a group who doctrines are at variance with the apostolic tradition the church had received (verses 4, 17–19), the group entering churches is sectarian having divided the church by rejecting its leadership (verse 8) and gathered a following of its own (verses 19, 22–23). Their motivation is partially financial gain (verses 11–12, 16). The description of them in verse 4, "certain intruders have stolen in among you," indicates that they may be itinerant prophets or teachers [others have called them apostates], *who are common in early Christianity. "Itinerant" prophets and preachers could often rely on the hospitality of their host church (1 Corinthians 9:14) and thus were in a position to misuse this privilege for financial gain (Romans 16:18). The contorted doctrines of some of these itinerants, coupled with their desire for gain, often posed problems for the churches they visited.*[9]

As such, the passage (verses 1–4) introduces and articulates the explicit purpose of the letter. The journey gives meaning for the reminder and commands that Jude passionately shares with the church in verses 5–24.

SECTION TWO

Looking at information that addresses cultural and sociological considerations relating to Jude is an excellent way to appreciate the original meaning of the text.

Cultural and Sociological Treasures of Jude

First we return to Jude, who saw himself as a servant or slave of Jesus Christ (verse 1). One of the main issues we need to keep in mind is the Mediterranean social system regarding humility. To get a feel of where Jude is coming from in his cultural background, we should remember—

> *The strategies for being humble include not presuming on others and avoiding even the appearance of lording it over another. Humble persons do not threaten or challenge another's rights, nor do they claim more for themselves than has been duly allotted them in life. They even stay a step below or behind their legal status.*[10]

Jude probably would have been alarmed to know that his readers in the modern Western world live in a culture where humility is frowned upon. Our culture encourages persons to flaunt their achievements and to state their "connections." As such, even for authority, Jude would have been reluctant to elevate himself. The example above is a good representation for appreciating the cultural mind-set and background from which Jude pens our text.

As previously stated, Jude would agree with the biblical worldview that God is in control of world history. As such, his readers would have understood that the circumstances that led to the writing of our passage were not unchangeable. He desired that his fellow believers love God and thereby reject evil. Jude was no weakling in his strict brand of Christianity, for he saw God as someone to take seriously. However, as a prophet he spoke from a heart of love and mercy.

In the Jewish culture of Jude, the biblical accounts of the Old Testament guided and established meaning and value for the society. Today our community seems to say that rationality and feelings should produce our morals. In our text we are encouraged, as were the initial readers, to believe that biblical values *can be lost by choice,* but it is the best and wisest thing to hold to God's ethical standards. Not only Jews but also all types of Gentiles should understand this truth.

Jude is saying that this brand of Christianity—

is being challenged by those who have rejected the teachings he follows and believes to be right. The structures that Jude operates by, such as good vs. evil and right vs. wrong, are challenged by a "transformational" process that seeks change. Thus, we see Jude fighting for his system, the one he believed is from God, and the one he wants to continue. . . His use of and adherence to the Old Testament and other Apocryphal books go unquestioned [but seek clarification today when teaching—author's comments]. . . .

Thus, Jude is a fighter and knows very well about how to carry on a war against threatened opposition. One of his main arguments is summed up with the following:

Central proposition—Don't deviate from the faith God gave us.

Reasoning—If you do, you will be under condemnation to hell.

Justification—Jesus, the apostles, the OT prophets, and Enoch clearly said so.[11]

The letter of Jude was written to many people who were still under the control of the Roman Empire (in which some emperors were viewed as gods). The Roman monetary system would have influenced economics for society. As conquered people, Jewish and Gentile readers of this letter still paid taxes to Rome. The false teachers in "ripping off" churches would seem not to fear outside intervention from Roman leaders. Further, no help would have been given by the elite Jewish establishment who had rejected the claims of Jesus Christ.

The persons to whom Jude was writing were generally people of modest means. Some could likely read and would have some measure of understanding when the letter was read in church gatherings. Jewish Christians had received their religious instruction mostly via oral tradition.

A personal observation from my background is how a letter in Bible times differs from how notes start and are conveyed in the modern era (very few messages are written today in mainstream ways). Jude encourages us to be militant or engage in active Christianity, whereas so often in our culture today we are preoccupied only with the love of God in both conversation and preaching. The church must repeatedly hear the "call to arms" that the gospel, once accepted, requires!

Choosing what is immoral and what is at the expense of the dictates of God's Scripture only devalues our Christian witness. The church today needs spiritual and moral revival from within.

SECTION THREE

Finally we gather the following scholarly and thoughtful information for enlightenment about our original text:

- Literary Background

- Theological Jewels

- Historical Exegesis of Jude—John Wesley

- Additional Notes of Value about Jude

Literary Background

The New Interpreter's Bible states about the literary background of Jude,

> *Jude is a genuine letter of mixed variety. Its deliberative rhetorical style classifies it as a paraenetic letter meant to advise and dissuade. The petition in verses 3–4 classifies it as a letter of request or petition. Jude's stated purpose is to persuade the church to "contend for the faith" (verse 3). This letter occupies a middle ground between documentary*

letters (e.g., personal, business) and literary letters written according to rhetorical conventions, and its structure is best described by discussing both genres. The letter begins with a typical Jewish-Christian prescript, introducing the sender and the recipients, followed by a blessing (verses 1–2).

Verses 3–4 are the body opening of the letter, which establishes common ground between the sender and the recipients—"contend for the faith that was once for all entrusted to the saints." The background of, or reason for, the petition follows in verse 4: ungodly false teachers have appeared in the Church, as was foretold in prophecy. Verse 3 corresponds to the rhetorical convention of exordium and verse 4 to narration; the exordium works to obtain the audience's goodwill and introduces the reason for the address; the narration gives the facts to explain the need for that address and to outline the main point(s) the remainder of the address will develop.[12]

Verses 1–4 of Jude represent a common theme in the whole Bible—that is, walking with God in all the light we have will require a spiritual and ethical fight against deception, hypocrisy, and compromise with sin. If our passage were omitted from this letter, we would lose the fundamental reason for the discourse that follows and the person who is writing. Having said this, the Bible as a whole would lose one of the sharpest pictures of the church of Christ under attack and the directly worded exhortation to "contend for the faith."

Klein, resolving the distinctly Jewish genre and interpretative techniques of Midrash found in Jude, says, "The effect was powerful, rhetorically, even if it seems troublesome to the modern reader. The harshness of Jude's polemic was mild by the standard of the day."[13]

One of the most fascinating literary considerations of Jude is its relation to 2 Peter. There are at least five explanations for the similarity of Jude (verses 4–19) and 2 Peter 2:1—3:3. Rose in the *Beacon Bible Commentary* says to this point,

> *1. Both epistles are from the same hand; 2. Each author—by divine inspiration—wrote independently of the other or any familiar source; 3. Jude borrowed from 2 Peter; 4. The author of 2 Peter borrowed from Jude; or 5. Entirely possible, each was dependent on a familiar source (no longer extant). Scholars have given the last three views serious consideration.*
>
> *While Charles Biggs argues for viewpoint number 3, J. B. Mayor defends number 4. Guthrie leaves this an unresolved literary problem with leanings toward viewpoint number 3. But Reicke*

holds view 5, assuming "a common tradition" that may well have been oral rather than written. The latter solution has much in its favor, especially viewed in the light of Jude 3–4 and 17. [Although very debatable, I lean to number 4, primarily due to considerations regarding the dating of each epistle.][14]

In closing this section, it is noteworthy to examine the nouns (mostly) found in verses 1–4; for example, *Jude, Jesus Christ*, and *God the Father* (verse 1), *beloved* (verse 3—particular importance for the author is seen later in the third sermon manuscript), and *certain intruders* (*men*—verse 4). A study of each adds light to our passage, but quite possibly the most important word for the reader is *appeal*, in verse 3 but translated literally as *exhorting* from the Greek. *Exhorting* represents a first continuous act that Jude authoritatively requires from his Christian brothers and sisters.

Theological Jewels

Some religious truths and implications are addressed by Jude throughout the letter. First note the emphasis on the lordship of Christ (verse 4—"[who is] our only Master"). In verse 3 we are asked to consider "the faith" that has been given to believers to fight for. What is that faith? In verse 1 Jude asks us to come to grips with our position in Christ as believers.

The *Beacon Bible Commentary* amplifies well the theological value and relevance of Jude when it says,

> From first to last Jude is Christ-centric. He builds, as all the apostles did, upon the one foundation, "our Lord Jesus Christ" (verses 1, 4, 17, 21, and 25). Climaxing his epistle on the note of "the only God our Savior (verse 25 ASV), he makes it amply clear that he is a Christian theist—God is one nature yet threefold in personality: Father (verse 1), Jesus Christ (verses 1, 4), and Holy Ghost (verse 20). Jude implies that "the only God" is Creator and Redeemer, Lawgiver and Judge of the whole universe. He is God of grace and glory (verses 4, 24), mercy and majesty (verses 2, 25), love and judgment (verses 2, 6, 15, 21), peace and power (verses 2, 25), salvation and destruction (verses 3, 5), and time and eternity (verses 4, 25). . . .[15]

The Christian life depends upon grace expressing itself in godliness—the very opposite of what errorists were doing (verses 4, 15–16, 18). First to Jude's whole theology is the inescapable relationship between belief and behavior, between error and evil, between sound faith and good works.

How relevant is Jude? In this generation with its defiance and denials of God (and Christ) and with its "new morality," nothing could be more relevant to our times. "As long as men need stern rebukes for their practices," writes Guthrie, "the epistle of Jude will remain relevant." Once more, it ought to become the fiery cross to rouse the soldiers to vigorous action against today's blatant apostasy.[16]

Theologically there is an explicit assumption that Jude's readers had a life-changing contact with God and had wholeheartedly received the Word as it had been preached and taught to them. The Jewish heritage of the readers helped their understanding of theological truths.

It has been roughly two thousand years since our text was penned, and it is eye-opening to consider how many times and in how many situations the problems confronted in this letter have raised their ugly head in the life of the church. In certain spiritual seasons Jude may be the most relevant and vital (even theologically) book in the Canon.

Historical Exegesis of Jude—John Wesley

In my research it often seems that Jude is a forgotten book. I felt that some of the thoughts by John Wesley about the text I am trying to expose are well worth writing down and remembering. The following is taken from the *One Volume New Testament Commentary*:

> [Verse 1—*Jude, a servant of Jesus Christ*] The highest glory which any, either angel or man, can aspire [is servanthood]. The word *servant* under the old covenant adapted to the spirit of fear and bond-

age that clave to that dispensation. When the time appointed of the Father came for the sending of His Son to redeem them that were under the Law, the word *servant* (used by the apostles concerning themselves and all children of God) signified one that, having the spirit of adoption, is made free by the Son of God. . . . "His servants shall serve Him" (Revelation 22:3). . . .

[Verse 1—*and kept safe for Jesus Christ*] So both the spring and accomplishment of salvation are pointed out. Security is premised, lest any of them should be discouraged by the terrible things which are afterward mentioned.

[Verse 3—*Beloved, while eagerly preparing to write to you about the salvation we share . . .*] Designed for all and enjoyed by all believers. Here the design of the epistle is expressed; the end of which correctly answers the beginning.

[Verse 4—*For certain intruders have stolen in among you, people who long ago were designated . . .*] Even as early as Enoch; of whom it foretold, that by their willful sins they would incur [verse 4—this condemnation as ungodly, who pervert the grace of our God . . .] revealed in the gospel.

[Verse 4—*into licentiousness*] into an occasion of more desperate wickedness.[17]

Additional Notes of Value about Jude

Verse 1—The distinctiveness of being a "servant" of Jesus Christ; "brotherhood" (whether physically or spiritually) does not mean that one is automatically a servant of Christ. The call of God is personal. In God's love the child of God is kept very secure for fellowship with Jesus Christ.

Verse 2—Mercy, peace, and love issue from being a servant of Jesus as the believer is kept safe in the love of God the Father. The life qualities of mercy, peace, and love are internal and exhibited externally with abundance.

Verse 3—All believers in Christ are "beloved." *Beloved* means we share a typical relationship with God through Jesus. There are no prejudices in the provisions of salvation. Walking with God means that the believer will be flexible to the leading of the Holy Spirit.

Verse 4—The battles of the Christian life (for the individual and the church) must involve our fight. Do not ignore prophecy in our journey of intimacy with Jesus.

The church must be alert to, and adamant against, false teaching and teachers. The church must remember the admonition of Bultmann to avoid "cheap grace." Simply put, being a servant of Jesus and maintaining a love relationship with God means "living clean" by the standards of the Word and maintaining an affirmative acceptance of the lordship of Christ in one's life.

Be aware of the following quote:

No one can ignore the amazing access most people have to the information made available through the Internet. From home computers to mobile [devices], we can post, read, and participate in the online world of digital media. For some, this tool of free exchange of ideas has become a new type of arena for private excitement and public execution. This is where ideology champions carry out their combat, cheered on by their virtual friends in the Social Media Coliseum.

Sadly, Church history is littered with the graves of those who died for having an "unacceptable faith." The fruit of this intolerance was the bloody persecution of those with different understanding, doctrines, or practices. Instead of copying the [methods] of our enemies who were trying to destroy the work of Christ by throwing the Christians into the Roman Coliseum, we should learn what it means to "contend earnestly for the faith which was once for all delivered to the saints."[18]

So many people are criticizing the weakness of the church, and the criticism is justified. Even people who are not Christians sense that something is wrong with the church. One reason for the gap is that there has not been a strong-enough central focus on the exact center of spiritual power in the pulpit.

We have not taught and preached enough on the tragedy of Calvary or the meaning of full redemption through the death and resurrection of Jesus Christ. We are referring to preaching without shame about the cross. That is the center of all meaningful Holiness preaching. I did not say teaching first about the effects of the cross but the center of power in the Christian faith, which is Jesus's death on Calvary and His resurrection from the grave on the third day.

Indeed, the center of all genuine Christianity is being authentic and faithful in all ways to the person of Jesus Christ. We fool only ourselves in thinking that Christianity is best based on following some insincere politician who says that he or she shares our values, personal convictions, and even a "homemade good conscience." If the church does not wake up to real and authentic holiness in America, we will become very dwarfed in redemptive value.

SECTION FOUR

Preaching the Word from the Text (Jude 1–4)

Remember that fruitful expository preaching applies the meaning of a passage gathered to applications that are important today for the lives of hearers (the second focus of this book). To expose Jude, one has to look widely to better appreciate the thought pattern of a writer in the first century to speak more authoritatively in the present generation.

In this section we are looking at "wise pearls" for the preacher. Three expository sermon examples from the same text in Jude follow:

- The theme for example one:
  The Holy Fight Involving All True Believers

- The theme for example two:
  The Clear and Present Dangers within the Church

- The theme for example three:
  The Beloved Church of Jesus

Wise Pearls for the Preacher

Who are you going to preach the Word of God to? Carefully reflect on your audience when preparing your sermon. Much of the hard work you have done in the preceding pages will be of little or no value or less fruitful if presented in the academic format illustrated in preparation for many congregations and groups.

The arrangement as to how you compile background research should be unique to you and "the flavor" preferred to draw from what is accumulated. Some texts may not even need the depth of exposure I have presented in previous pages, but I tried to cover reasonably thoroughly relevant data headings that give a framework for addressing research in preparing to speak the most important truths—the inspired Word of God.

It is time to break down and demonstrate what God is declaring to the people you are standing before. Present what you have been studying and researching in the most straightforward and easy-to-understand fashion possible. Get to know as much as possible the people sitting before you outside of the pulpit to communicate your delivery better.

In preparation you have been praying regularly and earnestly for God's will to be done in your preaching. No matter how busy your outside world is, pitch your tent for quiet times with God. As you prepare the actual Word, it is time to pray and fast even more, depending on the Holy Spirit. He is the architect for our lives, according to Jude 1:20–21. There is no substitute for intimacy with God to receive in a "fresh way" the anointing and unction of the Holy Spirit as you enter the pulpit. To try to camouflage the anointing of God is a dangerous exercise.

As you preach, having been diligent in full preparation, rely entirely on the Spirit of God to give the fruitfulness to the proclamation of the Word of God. Do not take shortcuts in preparing to preach, even when tempted. This goes for bivocational preachers also. Within the limitations of your time, order the priorities of your days with the help of the Holy Spirit. Many of my years as a preacher have been within important bivocational ministries in which many are called and allowed to serve.

Jude says, "But you, dear friends, as you build yourselves up in your most holy faith, praying in the Holy Spirit, keep yourselves in the love of God, waiting expectantly for the mercy of our Lord Jesus Christ for eternal life" (1:20–21 CSB). This means that the Holy Spirit is the planner or designer and constructs the disciple's life often gradually but with maturity, filling him or her with God's perfect love. A preacher then becomes a critical beacon light to warn and guide others against missing both the agony and the beauty of the cross and also about the constant danger that needs to avoided (see and meditate on Jude 21–23).

If you are speaking regularly to a group of people, I would suggest using a series of sermons related to a passage, chapter, or topic. Jude would be an excellent book from which to preach a five- or ten-week series of sermons. Consider preaching in series for your effectiveness and individual situation. You will never be able to share in one sermon all that you have diligently accumulated in your preparation.

Above all, live daily and come to the pulpit with a heart filled with God and His love. Remember: many obstacles and flooding waters cannot quench love (Song of Songs 8:7). The Holy Spirit in control of any disciple's life will awaken an inner passion that will fight insurmountable spiritual battles in this sinful world.

As you examine the following illustrative expository sermons, feel free to use them in any way for your preaching purposes. It is from your search for the original meaning of your text, complemented by your religious background and a practical understanding of the evil, dangerous, and chronic spiritual times in which we live, that you present the Word of God to hearers.

The prophetic Word must offer hope in the cross but also be "double-edged" in pointing out God's judgment on sinful attitudes and lifestyles from the Word. Preach without fear and with healthy reverence that you are the person representing God in the season and the hour. God has delivered you from sin in the conscious and unconscious levels of your life.

Be assured of this deep inner work of grace by the Holy Spirit and walk in all the light He gives you (see 1 John 1:7).

Be reminded that Jude, in the 25 verses shared in his letter, gives at least eight references to extraordinary characters and stories from the old covenant or testament. These include the Israelites' exodus from Egypt and going toward the promised land; the angels' rebellion in heaven; the sins of the people in Sodom and Gomorrah; facets from the lives of Cain, Balaam, Korah, and Enoch; and the angel Michael in a confrontation with the devil about the body of Moses (first taken from a book of the Apocrypha).

Why are the above facts relevant? No one can understand the messages correctly from Jude without an appreciation for and knowledge of the Old Testament illustrations used. On a broader scale to preachers—never stop in growing a more widespread recognition and understanding of the whole Canon. The Old and New Testaments work very well together, of course.

Also note that although I have prepared full manuscript sermons for illustrative purposes for the reader, I may not share in the actual discourse the full extent of what I have. When it comes to preaching, be open to whatever direction and changes the Holy Spirit provides. It is far more difficult for the Holy Spirit to work with someone who has not done his or her part faithfully in preparing well. Remember that the truths you have gleaned in your preparation can be of use for much more than one sermon.

There is an old story told in different formats about a new preacher querying someone in the congregation about how long he should preach that day. The person answered by saying he could teach and preach as long as he wanted—but after about twenty minutes the congregants' minds typically go to sleep. Remember to stay in touch as much as possible with how long a congregation can absorb a sermon. By the way, a funny story or statement may be an excellent way to bridge your initial contact with a gathering.

One of my many weak spots in preaching is coming up with a short and catchy topic or title for a sermon. Can I capture in a nutshell of three to seven words what the discourse will be about? It is good to be clear about this before entering the pulpit. Another weak spot I have when preparing to preach is a desire to run too fast with the idea God has given me. I want to run at my own pace after the getting His okay to proceed and do not return often enough to ask if my Lord is okay with the present place I am at in preparation. Listening to God intimately in the journey is so essential and overcomes unnecessary headaches that are often part of a preacher's life.

The spiritual gifts God gives to preachers to complement the giving of the Word are diverse and are not based on any one human model (except being Christlike in attitude and living a holy lifestyle). I have learned to be happy about the fact that God does not call just one type of personality and gifted person to preach. With all the gifts God gives you as

His called servant, use them all for the glory of God's kingdom. Never plan your life or any sermon without God's full input (Psalm 37:5).

Allow the Holy Spirit to be your all in all both in and out of the pulpit. You may be saying that you have too many imperfections in your brain and body to be an expository preacher. I have been there too. God made no mistake when He called you. He also entirely sanctified you. Do not downplay the perfect wisdom of God in choosing you. That is disrespectful to the Holy One.

> *The goal of faithfulness is not that we will do work for God, but that He will be free to do His work through us. God calls us to His service and places tremendous responsibilities on us. He expects no complaining on our part and does not explain His part. God wants to use us as He used His own Son.* (Oswald Chambers, *My Utmost for His Highest,* December 18 devotional)

As Jesus used five loaves of bread and two fish to feed the needs of people with complete satisfaction (see Matthew 14:13–21), He will take your whole life, gifts, and will, as inadequate and imperfect as you are, to feed the Word bountifully to God's children.

When God called you to preach He called you to be distinct, so do not try to make yourself into someone else. When you read the Old Testament Amos proclaiming the Word, you can see that he had his distinct style. The style of Peter the apostle was different. The powerful evangelistic sermons of Billy Graham were separate and distinct, and so was the particular delivery form of the apostle Paul. Each of those preachers was called and used separately and mightily by God.

God also yearns to use you mightily and with great fruitfulness as He sees best. Remember that many times these may not match the particular statistics of denominations and others.

God has called you, and He knows how best to use you, and I challenge you to be the best possible you can be in your preparation, delivery, and follow-up after preaching. Be genuine with the gifts and graces that have been given to you by God. Do not be a pretender by being merely an imitation of someone else.

There are three key points to always remember in preparing and delivery of your sermon:

1. Be practical in the applications you share.

2. Be practical in the applications you share.

3. Be practical in the applications you share.

In recent years the writings of Oswald Chambers have become a treasured storehouse for my soul. Where do you find a spiritual oasis for your life or literature that enriches outside of the Scriptures? Please listen carefully as the Holy Spirit speaks through thoughts that I could not express better:

We have to realize that we cannot earn or win anything from God through our efforts. We must either receive it as a gift or do without it. The greatest spiritual blessing we receive is when we come to the knowledge that we are destitute. Until we get there, our Lord is powerless. He can do nothing for us as long as we think we are sufficient in and of ourselves. We must enter into His kingdom through the door of poverty. As long as we are "rich," particularly in the area of pride or independence, God can do nothing for us. It is when we get hungry spiritually that we receive the Holy Spirit. The gift of the essential nature of God is placed and made effective in us by the Holy Spirit. He imparts to us the quickening life of Jesus, making us truly alive. He takes that which was "beyond" us and places it "within" us. And immediately, once "the beyond" has come "within," it rises to "the above," and we are lifted into the kingdom where Jesus lives and reigns. (Oswald Chambers, *My Utmost for His Highest*, November 28 devotional)

If you preach only your personal experiences, so much of the heart of the gospel will be lost. All genuine believing faith is solidified on God's revealed truth. *Expose God's revealed truth* made known in the Bible.

As much as is possible, be upbeat and jovial in the flow of your thoughts through your sermon. Remember: It is harder to listen to a "statue" in the pulpit, even if your content is superb. There are diverse ways to introduce and conclude a sermon. This book is not about general constructions for your presentation. Therefore, my only encouragement is to be pointed and succinct in your introduction and conclusion of the preached Word.

Also, when using illustrations in your sermons from other people, remember to give appropriate credit or attention. We will now illustrate three different and original expository sermons in a manuscript format using Jude 1–4 as our text for each.

SERMON ONE

The Holy Fight Involving All True Believers

Objective or Purpose: To teach the enormity and the relevance of the fight Jude requires from God's children

Note: I am of the trend of thought that sometimes the objective and topic for an expository sermon may not finally germinate until the preacher is actually working on the address.

Theme: The Holy Fight Involving All True Believers

Text: Jude 1–4, using the Christian Standard Bible (CSB):

> *Jude, a servant of Jesus Christ and a brother of James:*
>
> *To those who are the called, loved by God the Father and kept for Jesus Christ.*
>
> *May mercy, peace, and love be multiplied to you.*
>
> *Dear friends, although I was eager to write you about the salvation we share, I found it necessary to write, appealing to you to contend for the faith that was delivered to the saints once for all. For some people, who were designated for this judgment long ago, have come in by stealth; they are ungodly, turning the grace of our God into sensuality and denying Jesus Christ, our only Master and Lord.*

Introduction: Living in intimacy with God according to Jude is walking with God in all the light we have and will require a spiritual and ethical fight against deception, hypocrisy, and compromise with sin.

What is the appreciation we should have about the salvation of one's soul according to the Bible and supported by the man of God, Jude? It means one's redemption from sin includes changes in your daily behavior—your lifestyle has dramatically changed. You no longer look at things in the same way on the inside or in your outward actions. Ongoing brand-new Christlike virtues are now a part of you.

Are your desires new? Have the old things that rivaled God lost their power to attract you? One of the specified tests for determining if the work of salvation is real and Jesus is your Savior is this: Has God changed the things that mattered to you?

If you still yearn for the old things before deliverance as Lot's wife did in the Old Testament, wanting to return to the sinful lifestyle of Sodom and Gomorrah, it is foolish to testify to being a believer in Christ. Do not deceive yourself. As you receive salvation from sin, the Spirit of God makes the change very evident in your life and thoughts.

And when pitfalls and adversity come, you will be amazed by the incredible difference in you. You now have a "shameless audacity" to love Jesus without apology. The Holy Spirit has given you personal assurance that all is well between you and Jesus.

That is why Paul says clearly, and Jude would entirely agree as you read his 25 verses—"If anyone is in Christ, he is a new creation; old things have passed away; behold, all things have become new" (2 Corinthians 5:17 NKJV).

We must answer three questions today about "contending for the fight" that Jude speaks about in verse 3: Who calls us to fight? For whom is the challenge to fight? What is the central focus of the fight?

1. Who calls us to fight?

A. A loving servant of Christ (v. 1)

Jude is the author of this letter, a "submitted person" found in the definition of *doulos,* the Greek word for *slave* or *servant* that the Bible speaks of. Thus, the author's "lived world" is organized by his submission to his faith system. The organized lived world points Jude in the direction of being dependent upon the care and love of God, having a stable, ethical standard of right vs. wrong, good vs. evil, and having a strong vision about the future.

A loving servant is hungry for the return of Jesus Christ. Jude, the holy servant of Christ, is calling the church to fight.

Jude is a spiritual person who loved God and hated evil. Jude had faith in God and knew our Lord was in control of everything.

Here was a loving servant amid a season in which the early church faced great persecution and uncertainty. In these initial years after the resurrection of Jesus, the new church suffered in a hostile Roman world government. It was a hostile environment in which to carry out the mission commanded by Jesus Christ.

Jude was living as God's slave, as Peter had directed in 1 Peter 2:16—"Live as free people, but do not use your freedom as a cover-up for evil; live as God's slaves" (NIV).

B. A person with significant authority (v. 1)

i. Jude was one of the brothers of Jesus Christ (see Matthew 13:55; Mark 6:3). The latter verse says, "'Isn't this the carpenter, the son of Mary, and the brother of James, Joses, Judas [Jude], and Simon? And aren't his sisters here with us?' So they were offended by him."

ii. Jude was also the brother of the first leader of the church at the home church in Jerusalem, and we are referring to James—another brother of Jesus. The man writing to us had a lot of "clout" but used his authority with a deeply sensed aura of humility from his writings.

2. For whom is the challenge to fight?

Two days before the independence of Jamaica, West Indies, in 1962 a remarkable boxing match took place at the newly built National Stadium in Kingston. The late Bunny Grant was then the lightweight and welterweight boxing champion of Jamaica and got the opportunity to fight the then-Commonwealth lightweight champion, England's Dave Charnley. In August 1962 Bunny fought "out of his skin"—exceptionally well—and won the boxing match, giving Jamaica a remarkable independence gift. It was seen as a truly historic occasion that symbolically cut the ties with British colonial rule.

For the next fifty years after that fight, Bunny continued to say that he had fought for the joy of Jamaicans and knew for whom he was struggling. He had not entered the ring on his own behalf. Indeed, that night was a remarkable independence gift to Jamaicans.

Jude was not asking for a boxing match, but he was clear in whom he was calling to get into a real holy fight. Are you among the Christians or disciples Jude is speaking to today? All genuine Christians are daily involved in spiritual warfare or fighting.

"'Not by might nor by power, but by my Spirit,' says the Lord Almighty" (Zechariah 4:6 NIV).

Jude would agree with the encouragement of "fighting another round" (made famous by "Gentleman Jim" Corbett, one of the first American heavyweight boxing champions of the world).

Years ago I pastored in an all-Indian community. A young lady had gloriously received Jesus as her personal Savior and Lord and in so doing had given up walking the way of the Islamic religion. It was now time this Sunday morning for her water baptism in front of the community. A person who had been close to this new Christian was angry at me for being the Christian minister who had spiritually nurtured her, and he came determined to beat me up physically on the morning of her baptism. Thank goodness, the Spirit of Lord helped me escape that fight. But it was not even that type of conflict Jude is writing about.

Therefore, who is the believer the text speaks of?

A. Believers who are called and loved by God (v. 1)

 i. "You did not choose [call] me, but I chose [called] you. I appointed you to go and produce fruit and that your fruit should remain" (John 15:16).

 ii. "As the Father has loved me, I have also loved you. Remain in my love" (John 15:9).

iii. Jude, the disciple, is speaking for Jesus Christ, who wants our absolute, unrestricted devotion to the Lord of Lords and King of Kings. Total surrender and submission belong wholly to God. Are you residing in the Savior and linked without reservations to Him?

B. Believers who are kept by Jesus Christ (v. 1)

On some occasions taking my youngest daughter, Casey, as a child to the doctor and having her blood drawn was like World War III. Sometimes she had to be held so the nurse could draw the blood. I knew Casey was trying in different ways to say that there must be another way other than the pain and fear she felt about giving blood. But as her father I was sorry because there was no other way to get the needed blood results so that she could be treated appropriately for her illness. I could not take away the fear and pain of the sticks and needles, but I could offer my continued presence with her during the procedures.

I share the illustration about Casey while first remembering Jesus in the Garden of Gethsemane as a human, asking His Father on three occasions (see Matthew 26:36–46) for a different way other than going through a painful death on the cross. It broke the Heavenly Father's heart to see His beloved Son in such human agony and knew He could not help because our salvation for every sin depended on Jesus's obedience in going to Calvary to suffer greatly and die on the cross.

Second, in a similar way those who have decided to follow the direction of the cross wholeheartedly in a life of suffering and adversity are promised that Jesus keeps His children well. Hallelujah! "Share in suffering like a good soldier of Christ Jesus" (2 Timothy 2:3).

C. Blessed believers in heavenly abundance (v. 2)

Mercy, peace, and love are multiplied for believers in Christ. You are to be highly favored, and with that privilege come primary spiritual responsibilities.

3. What is the central focus of the fight?

A. Contend vigorously and earnestly.

i. Believers must be involved in the fight Jude is asking us to focus on. If not, we lose our authority and mandate as disciples. The individual believer may well lose his or her salvation if he or she does not get involved in the fight. This need to fight is the premise upon which Jude appeals to the body of Christ.

ii. How relevant is Jude? In this generation with so many showing defiance against and denial of God (and Christ as the only Savior), with its "new morality," nothing is more relevant to our times. "As long as men need stern rebukes for their practices," writes theologian Guthrie, "the epistle of Jude will remain relevant." Once more it ought to become "the fiery cross to rouse the soldiers to vigorous action against today's blatant apostasy."

iii. Today materialism and racism have gotten into many people in the church of Christ. If this pathetic behavior continues, we have lost our voice and "salt" to lift up Christ and to be a source of hope in this messed-up world.

B. Go against immoral men who have sneaked into the church—these unholy people must face a holy fight by God's loving family.

i. The enemy highlighted is a severe impediment to the body of Christ. It has been roughly two thousand years since our text was written, and it is eye-opening to consider how repeatedly the problems confronted in this letter have raised their ugly heads in the life of the church. In certain spiritual seasons, Jude may be the most important and essential book in the Canon.

Christian apologetics is a needed branch of Christian theology or daily living that defends Christianity against objections like what Jude warns of and much more.

ii. The freely impulsive, unholy sexual living and money-grabbing encouraged by people who have stealthily entered the church require us as the church to stand against these dangers.

iii. Preach, teach, and speak out without fear against the lifestyle of these immoral people touting their horns as "God's people." We are going up against high, unholy people who are supported by "spiritual forces of evil in the heavenly places" (see Ephesians 6:12). But in Christ we are overcomers and victorious.

Conclusion: Some fights for God's children are to be only in the hands of God. As 2 Chronicles 20:15 says, "The battle is not yours, but God's" (CSB).

But Jude is referring to a battle in which we are co-laborers with Jesus against immorality and evildoers among God's church and people. Let our watchword be 2 Corinthians

7:1—"Since we have these promises, let us cleanse ourselves from every impurity of the flesh and spirit, bringing holiness to completion in the fear of God" (CSB). Let others see real Christlike love in our midst.

C. S. Lewis wrote a gem that I treasure: "The true Christian's nostril is to be continually attentive to the inner cesspool." Some cesspools are all around us, and our spiritual eyes and ears must be attentive and refuse to play along. We need to get all unrighteousness out of our midst if such people will not repent and turn in full brokenness to Christ. We are in a holy war that we dare not lose.

Remember some of the last words from the apostle Paul to the elders of the church at Ephesus—

> *I declare to you today that I am innocent of the blood of any of you. For I have not hesitated to proclaim to you the whole will of God. Keep watch over yourselves and all the flock of which the Holy Spirit has made you overseers. Be shepherds of the church of God, which he bought with his own blood. I know that after I leave, savage wolves will come in among you and will not spare the flock. Even from your own number men will arise and distort the truth in order to draw away disciples after them. So be on your guard! Remember that for three years I never stopped warning each of you night and day with tears.* (Acts 20:26–31 NIV)

These words of Paul are pertinent, relevant, and compelling today.

Our greatest weapon is the infilling of the Holy Spirit and the mighty power He gives each child who is in one accord with Him and His will. Does the Holy Spirit fully empower you and love through you for the spiritual war that we cannot avoid?

Someone has said that there are no "demilitarized zones" in the spiritual warfare that must be fought and won by God's church. You are either on God's side (His church) or the side of the devil and his followers. Whose eternal report are you going to believe and follow?

You are challenged to believe the report of Jesus's love servant Jude. He says these days are dire and that we need to go where the devil fights and eradicate his camp. Are you a holy warrior willing to follow Jesus everywhere and without reservation?

The ruler of the kingdom of God reigns supreme, and it is an honor and privilege to travel through life with Jesus, even if it means our deaths. Let us *live* and *die* to fight for Jesus even in the darkest and most insecure places. Satan's kingdom must come down, says one songwriter. In the cross your past, your future, and your present are secure in the hands of Jesus.

We must *count the cost* now as we face our tomorrows and as the inevitable return of Jesus for His real church draws closer and closer. Promise God that you will pay the price to belong continually to Jesus and His church.

SERMON TWO

The Clear and Present Dangers within the Church

Objective or Purpose: To teach the enormity of some of the ungodly and immoral persons coming into the church and the damage these men and women can cause among the faithful.

Topic: The Clear and Present Dangers within the Church

Text: Jude 1–4, using the Christian Standard Bible (See Sermon One for text.)

Introduction: Jude is a fighter and knows very well how to carry on a war against threatening opposition in the body of Christ. One of his main arguments is summed up with the following thought pattern by Turner:

The central proposition to be wholly engrained in us—Don't deviate from the faith God gave us through our belief in the death and resurrection of Jesus Christ.

The profound reasoning—If you do not fight in spiritual warfare, you are in deep trouble spiritually and can lose your soul even after starting well in Christ.

Justification—Jesus, the apostles, the Old Testament prophets, and back to Enoch clearly provided examples about spiritual warfare. Do not joke around with the enemies within our ranks who pose as God's children.

What was the occasion for the letter?

It was the infiltration of the church by a group of people whose doctrines and lifestyles were at variance with the apostolic tradition the church had received. These people had already divided the church by rejecting its leadership (v. 8) and gathered a following of their own (vv. 19, 22–23). Their motivation was partially financial gain (vv. 11–12, 16).

The description of them in verse 4, "certain intruders have stolen in among you," indicates that they may be itinerant prophets or teachers but opposite the gospel in their teaching, which was common in early Christianity.

Itinerant prophets and preachers could rely on the hospitality of their host church (see 1 Corinthians 9:14) and thus were in a position to misuse this privilege for financial gain. "For such people are not serving our Lord Christ, but their appetites. By smooth talk and flattery they deceive the minds of naive people" (Romans 16:18 NIV).

The contorted doctrines of some of these travelers, coupled with their desire for gain, often posed problems for the churches they visited.

Hear and respond well to the Word of God today where it says, "Open my eyes that I may see wonderful things in your law [the Word of God]" (Psalm 119:18 NIV).

1. The danger indicated by Jude is a clear and present jeopardy today.

I hear some saying that what happened in the early church during the time of Jude cannot happen today in the 21st-century church. Our regular, everyday human relationships are the very situations in which the holy life of God are to be exhibited for the glory of God.

It is within these circumstances that the devil tries to come and use "hypocritical people" or transit false prophets to destroy God's people and Christian fellowship.

I ask you to listen carefully to some things that happened to Ann and me many years ago in our early ministry. Please be wiser and quicker to fathom the slippery ways that our greatest enemy, the devil, tries to intervene in our lives.

A. In our first assignment after leaving college, we had the privilege of planting a Church of the Nazarene in Mandeville, Jamaica, West Indies. We had been married just a year and had no children. We were filled with Holy Spirit enthusiasm and yearned to make an impact for Christ in this vital city on the island. The church had bought a former relatively small radio studio property that included a comfortable home.

During our visits in the community, we came across a well-spoken-looking gentleman whom we will call "Mr. Brown" who visited our worship services. As we interacted with him, we heard him give his testimony and a number of illustrations from his past life that seemed genuine. Also, we gathered that he was having difficulty communicating with his wife and was trying to straighten out his home problems.

He asked if he could stay with us a few days. We had an empty room off from the main house, and it seemed okay. We tried to make contact with his wife as soon as possible. He appeared to be attending to his problems and was not staying in his room during the daytime.

Within a few days we were contacted by a late-childhood friend and mentor from a nearby city who had been contacted by Mr. Brown, supposedly representing me. My friend was a lawyer and informed me that I "was borrowing some money for a good deal." Mr. Brown obviously understood that I knew this lawyer through someone else.

If not for the grace of God and caring communication by my lawyer friend and mentor, I could have eventually been in trouble for fraud and misrepresentation. Our ministry would have been soiled before starting. By the way, during those few days Mr. Brown had gone as far as Kingston, over fifty miles away, to try a similar scheme involving a family member.

We later found out from Mr. Brown's wife that this slippery deception was something he had tried at other churches and had gotten into trouble with the law.

Here was someone using the privilege extended by kindness, hospitality, and compassion for obtaining financial gain. Sounds so much like the people Jude referred to in his letter.

In our text we are encouraged, as were the initial readers, to believe that bad choices can lose biblical values for a holy life. It is the best and wisest thing to hold to God's ethical standards. Jude verses 11–13 says, "Woe to them! For they have gone the way of Cain, have plunged into Balaam's error for profit, and have perished in Korah's rebellion. These people are dangerous reefs at your love feasts as they eat with you without reverence. They are shepherds who only look after themselves. They are waterless clouds carried along by winds; trees in late autumn—fruitless, twice dead and uprooted" (CSB).

Love in practical ways the needy and disenfranchised, but keep a watchful eye for the deceitful who will attempt to hurt the church. These deceitful come not only from hypocritical preachers and teachers but also politicians who pretend to have faith but live lives that are entirely opposite of what the Word of God instructs.

Some years later while planting another Nazarene church at a converted storefront building in Cambria Heights, Queens, New York, I received a phone call from someone visiting from a Caribbean island claiming to be a long-time Nazarene who was a brain surgeon on a particular assignment to New York on behalf of the named Caribbean government at one of the leading New York City hospitals. I will refer to this person as "Dr. Smith." He needed a Nazarene church home while in the city and chose ours. He began attending faithfully except for times when he had medical calls.

He spoke well about his spirituality growing up in one of our Sunday Schools back home and had been good worship leader there. He even mentioned someone I knew from my college days in Trinidad years before, a roommate of mine (he did not know this at the time he mentioned the person).

The problem was this—after one or two months one of the ladies in the congregation came to me for advice about the bachelor, Dr. Smith, who seemed to be showing romantic interest in her. I knew he was also showing interest in another young lady who was a new convert at that time.

I decided to call the roommate he had mentioned whom he did not know I was already acquainted with from my college days. My friend was still pastoring there and was kind enough to share useful information.

First, Dr. Smith had indeed grown up in church and was a recently married policeman with a new child a home. When I then called "Dr./Policeman" Smith, a lady picked up the phone, claiming to be another wife. I never heard from that gentleman again. How utterly far from the faith this man had come!

You can imagine the immorality he could have quickly spread in our growing congregation if it were not for the grace and intervention of God.

2. The danger that infiltrates has diverse ways of showing its ugly head, says Jude.

A. Jude 5—Falling into *unbelief* like the people of God who had been delivered from Egypt but then went back into disbelief. Tony Reinke is right when he says, "Unbelief is our Kryptonite," in the Christian walk. The proclaimed truth of God's Word is the urgent need for His people.

B. Jude 6—Falling into *pride* like the fallen angels in heaven, who wanted to have a place that God did not intend. "For a day belonging to the Lord of Armies is coming against all that is proud and lofty, against all that is lifted up—it will be humbled" (Isaiah 2:12 CSB). The truth proclaimed is the needed Word to God's people.

C. Jude 7—Falling into *sexual immorality and wicked perversions* like the unholy people of the Old Testament cities of Sodom and Gomorrah (see Genesis 19). "For this is God's will, your sanctification: that you keep away from sexual immorality, that each of you knows how to control his own body in holiness and honor, not with lustful passions, like the Gentiles, who don't know God. This means one must not transgress against and take advantage of a brother or sister in this manner, because the Lord is an avenger of all these offenses, as we also previously told and warned you. For God has not called us to impurity but to live in holiness." (1 Thessalonians 4:3–7 CSB) The truth proclaimed is the authoritative Word to God's people. Too many men and women have covered sexual sins in and out of the church. It is time for all sex offenders to come clean and to receive forgiveness and redemption through God's grace.

D. Judgment is coming, and it will start first in the church. Listen and obey the Word so that you do not miss heaven. Your sex life and sinful passions need to be entirely in Jesus's hands; commit to a humble walk with Jesus and walk by faith in the invisible hand of our Savior and Lord.

Conclusion: We face people who come against the church who often rely on their dreams—defile their flesh, reject authority, and notably slander those in the body of Christ (Jude 8). In the church are too many dark and blemished spots.

I love listening and singing to Ron Kenoly (the artist's name some young people may not know) leading in worship as the church sings praises to Jesus. But we need to realize what will negate our singing praises to Jesus. A significant hindrance is the failure to deal with the unholy folly that too often arises in the church by flawed and hypocritical people.

Remember well Hebrews 6: 1–3: "Let us leave the elementary teaching about Christ and go on to maturity, not laying again a foundation of repentance from dead works, faith in God, teaching about ritual washings, laying on of hands, the resurrection of the dead, and eternal judgment. And we will do this if God permits" (CSB).

May each listener of the Word of God receive personally these words of Christ: "Sanctify them by the truth; your word is truth" (John 17:17 CSB). Jesus is the only source for our full deliverance and power to fight and overcome the clear and present dangers within the church. Onward, Christian soldiers—stand up and be proud to be counted faithful in your role in the body of Christ. Report to duty for Jesus!

It is time for you to fully support Jesus's revival fires that are needed to destroy the camps of the devil thoroughly. Call upon Jesus for full salvation and go forward without fear. Hallelujah!

SERMON THREE

The Beloved Church of Jesus

Objective or Purpose: To give a working and realistic definition of the church. Further, to emphasize the holy makeup and function of the church of Jesus Christ today.

Topic: The Beloved Church of Jesus

Text: Jude 1–4 (NRSV)

> *Jude, a servant of Jesus Christ and brother of James, To those who are called, who are beloved in God the Father and kept safe for Jesus Christ: May mercy, peace, and love be yours in abundance. Beloved, while eagerly preparing to write to you about the salvation we share, I find it necessary to write and appeal to you to contend for the faith that was once for all entrusted to the saints. For certain intruders have stolen in among you, people who long ago were designated for this condemnation as ungodly, who pervert the grace of our God into licentiousness and deny our only Master and Lord, Jesus Christ.*

Introduction: Who are the beloved that Jude speaks of in verses 1 and 3? He is speaking about Christ's church or God's holy and beautiful church. One way to understand the functioning church is found in 1 Peter 2:9–10: "You are a chosen race, a royal priesthood, a holy nation, God's people, so that you may proclaim the mighty acts of him who called you out of darkness into his marvelous light. Once you were not a people, but now you are God's people; once you had not received mercy, but now you have received mercy."

Jude gives another view of God's church in verses 1–3, describing a practical and productive lifestyle for disciples that is to be emulated today.

Remember: "Your word is a lamp for my feet and a light on my path" (Psalm 119:105 CSB).

In his letter Jude is getting the word out that all members of Christ's church must be faithful to His will as God's people at any cost and sacrifice. This should bring great joy and reverence among God's children. We are part of an unshakeable kingdom, and the only door to eternal life, through Christ, is not to be taken lightly—but is the substance of our most holy faith, says the writer of our text. God's children have a peerless position in Christ as members of His militant and "great commissioned" church.

Often the words of a beautiful and holy hymn say it far better than I can. The refrain of "A Glorious Church," written by Ralph E. Hudson, says,

> 'Tis a glorious Church without spot or wrinkle,
>   Washed in the blood of the Lamb.
> 'Tis a glorious Church without spot or wrinkle,
>   Washed in the blood of the Lamb.

Being a part of Christ's church means being wholly identified with Jesus, our Lord. This relationship with Christ says you are free from sin from the very core of your being as seen in your positive attitude and ethical lifestyle. It is this precious relationship with Jesus that the writer Jude asks us to protect and proclaim with a great passion.

The church is described as God's *beloved* (or *dear friends*) by Jude. Who is beloved?

A. People who are servants of Christ—"a servant of Jesus Christ" (v. 1)

As a member of God's church, Jude refers to himself with great joy as a servant of Christ or His love slave. Jude first challenges one of the Greek ideals of "freedom" by calling himself a "slave." We need to see Jude as a radical person within Greek and Hebrew society. In other words, this Christian has taken a stand against the standard mode of existence. We also see Jude as a social radical who rejects the Greek ideal of freedom in favor of submitting himself as a voluntary slave to his Lord and Savior, Jesus Christ. Hallelujah! We see this exemplified in the very life of Jesus lived as a radical and perfect human in life and ministry. The church today must practically imitate—

i. The humility and serving spirit of Jesus as He washed the feet of Peter and the other disciples (John 13:1–17).

ii. Jesus reaching across cultural and other backgrounds. He reached out to people who were not "supposed" to be like Him or were not the kind whom Jews were to show special interest in, such as Samaritans, women, religious leaders, and the poor. The genuine, holy church lives that lifestyle just as Jesus did.

B. People secure in Christ: "To those who are called, who are beloved in God the Father and kept safe for Jesus Christ" (v. 1).

i. Jesus says, "My sheep hear my voice . . . and they follow me" (John 10:27). They follow Him wholeheartedly.

ii. The church loves Jesus without reservation and obeys God (see John 14:15).

C. People satisfied in Christ: "May mercy, peace, and love be yours in abundance" (v. 2).

i. More heaven-sent abundance is promised. Jesus said in John 10:10, "I came that they may have life, and have it abundantly." In God's right hand there are pleasures always, says the psalmist (Psalm 16:11).

ii. God offers all the best to His disciples. Jesus fills His children—and not halfheartedly. Being filled with the Holy Spirit is both the promise and the encouragement for His church (Ephesians 5:18).

D. People saved from sin by Christ: "The salvation we share . . ." (v. 3).

What does Jude mean by the real, blood-washed salvation we share as the beloved of Christ?

God does forgive, but it cost the breaking of His heart with grief in the death of Jesus Christ to enable Him to do so. The great miracle of the grace of God is that He forgives sin, and it is the death of Jesus Christ alone that enables the divine nature to forgive and to remain true to itself in doing so. It is shallow nonsense to say that God forgives us because He is love. Once convicted of sin, we will never repeat this. The love of God means Calvary— nothing less! The love of God is spelled out on the Cross and nowhere else. The only basis for which God can forgive me is the Cross of Christ. It is there that His conscience is satisfied. (Oswald Chambers, *My Utmost for His Highest*, November 19 devotional)

Being saved from sin (our glorious salvation) means a new relationship with Christ, and this new fellowship is distinct and set apart from ungodly living. When we look at many parts of today's American church with its behavior and political leanings, we have to wonder how many church people have actually been to the cross and washed in the blood of the Lamb. How many evangelical people take the cross of Jesus very seriously?

In examining the writings of Jude, I am deeply troubled in what we see in too many parts of the church in the United States. We are a country in need of many more people with holy hearts and behavior. Our country needs to understand that we face the conviction of the Holy Spirit for our sins as a nation, and we must first look within our hearts in the church. We need more church people who understand first that we are servants.

We are to be called-out people who ask God to sustain healthy ethical and moral choices given by His wisdom in big and small matters. A clean and healthy people is our Savior's requirement for His church.

Without a spiritual and moral revival in the land of America, we'll continue destroying what God has given to us. Our favor from God is steadily going to the grave, and we will shrink to nothing if the church does not awake and move forward in obedience to the guidance and power of God.

E. People who are saints or holy followers of Christ: "For the faith that was once for all entrusted to the saints" (v. 3).

"I have no right to say I believe in God unless I order my life as under His all-seeing Eye" (Oswald Chambers, *The Quotable Oswald Chambers* [Grand Rapids: Discovery House, 2011], 26). *The person who orders his or her life according to Christ and His Word is the type of saint God requires.*

The presence of a saint is the holiness that pleases God and brings Him the glory in this life and takes us triumphantly into our home in heaven. Praise the Lord!

The power and infilling of the Holy Spirit in the saint's life provide that guarantee and a shameless audacity to love God through everything in this life. That is Christ's church. God has entrusted you as saints with holy matters to attend to.

Conclusion: Are you a part of the church family or the beloved that Jude requires in our text?

In the great hymn "I Surrender All" we read these words:

All to Jesus I surrender;
  All to Him I freely give.
I will ever love and trust Him,
  In His presence daily live.

All to Jesus I surrender;
  Humbly at His feet I bow,
Worldly pleasures all forsaken.
  Take me, Jesus, take me now.

All to Jesus, I surrender;
  Make me, Savior, wholly Thine;
Let me feel the Holy Spirit;
  Truly know that Thou art mine.

Verses 1–4 of Jude represent a common theme and framework for the whole Bible. That is, walking with God in all the light we have will require us as the church of Jesus to engage in a spiritual and ethical fight against deception, hypocrisy, and compromise with sin.

Do you need to come to the cross to receive the grace that will cement your place in the holy church that the Bible speaks about in our text? Within Christ's church His power is far higher and more powerful than everything that comes against His people.

Among the many obstacles we face are drugs, illicit sex, despair, physical handicaps, an inclination to suicide, depression caused by financial pressure, lies, and much more. You name your heavy burden, and Jesus will deliver you and give you every aspect of power needed to be holy from the core of your being in an ungodly world. God is bigger than any obstacle you can experience, both seen and unseen. Enter into and live joyfully by faith in the victorious church and family of Jesus. Let the peace of Jesus fill your soul.

The beloved church of Jesus is holy, beautiful, and powerful. It is within this church, people saved soley by the blood of Jesus and embued with His resurrection power, that we can respond effectively to our Commander's order to be spiritually militant in this life with the glorious promise of heaven as our reward. Now is the time to be on fire for Jesus.

Abandon your lives in God's plan for you and the directions given in the Word of God. Wake up, church! Reach out with hearts of Christ's love, demonstrated on the cross, to the poor, hungry, disenfranchised, and dying in sin and going to hell. Do not be involved in any movement or follow any person who detracts from Jesus Christ.

Concluding Thoughts

I genuinely hope that this illustrative journey into expository Holiness preaching has been a blessing and also been thought-provoking. At the very minimum, it is my prayer that each reader is challenged to an upward view in his or her heart and spiritual reflection. Remember: expository preaching is often hard work, but the benefits are beyond my ability to positively explain.

Expository preaching is exciting and very needed in the body of Christ. Be patient and gentle with yourself in developing your graphic preaching skills. Practicing it will bring you steady progress in the pulpit. Remember that in informative or expository presentations you are focusing on the best meaning of the text and the applications that come from within—not a topic first and foremost and then finding parallel biblical passages to support it.

Using the first four verses of Jude, three useable sermons have been prepared and presented. Each message is distinct, but all of them are nurtured from diligently searching for the original meaning of the text. Needless to say from the research of Jude, many more sermons on the same verses could be voiced with divine authority.

I sincerely believe that many readers of my limited study of the book Jude could prepare far better presentable expository sermons from what is illustrated. Go for it!

Also, be reminded that in reflecting on the explanations of Jude 1–4, you have a reservoir of spiritual truths that will be helpful when presenting applications from other passages.

CONCLUSION

The Clear Value of the Altar Call

It is now essential to focus a few thoughts about the importance of favorable altar calls after delivering the Word of God. Why? Consider the preacher as a good salesperson for the Lord, much like a salesperson who sometimes does not know how to get the person being sold a product to sign the contract after the completing of the transaction. It is indeed the Holy Spirit alone who deals with, convicts, and prompts the hearts of listeners, who gives any eternal fruit to the Word of God. But as a preacher, you are a called co-laborer with Christ who needs to do everything available for the best "field" on which the Holy Spirit can provide fruit through grace via the cross.

Getting a response from listeners is an essential key to our preaching. The Word of God is preached so that a listener can answer a genuine yes to the shared Word. That responsive yes can come through the lifting of a hand, the bowing of the head, going forward to an altar for prayer, or some other human way guided by the Holy Spirit. If you sense that an opportunity for public response is best after preaching, plan for it and avoiding treating it as a random afterthought.

> *The only ground on which God can forgive our sin and reinstate us to His favor is through the Cross of Christ. There is no other way! Forgiveness, which is so easy for us to accept, cost the agony at Calvary. We should never take the forgiveness of sin, the gift of the Holy Spirit, and our sanctification in simple faith, and then forget the enormous cost to God that made all of this ours. Forgiveness is the divine miracle of grace. The cost to God was the Cross of Christ. To forgive sin, while remaining a holy God, this price had to be paid. Never accept a view of the fatherhood of God if it blots out the atonement."* (Oswald Chambers, *My Utmost for His Highest*, November 20 devotional)

Any choice to grow in grace by the listener to the Word is made possible only through the provisions of the cross. Remember the words of 1 Corinthians 1:18—"The message about the cross is foolishness to those who are perishing, but to us who are being saved it is the power of God."

The apostle Paul speaks about sharing the good news of the gospel of the cross:

> *Most of the brothers have gained confidence in the Lord from my imprisonment and dare even more to speak the word fearlessly. To be sure, some preach Christ out of envy and rivalry, but others out of good will. These preach out of love, knowing that I am appointed for the defense of the gospel; the others proclaim Christ out of selfish ambition, not sincerely, thinking that they will cause me trouble in my imprisonment. What does it matter? Only that in every way, whether from false motives or true, Christ is proclaimed, and in this I rejoice. Yes, and I will continue to rejoice.* (Philippians 1:14–18 CSB)

As an expository preacher, you (and any other type of presenter) share the gospel, I trust, from true motives and intentions, and this brings great rejoicing in the halls of heaven. Therefore, go the last mile of the way and challenge listeners to respond to the Word and not just be satisfied with listening to a good sermon.

When giving an altar call be clear and straightforward in what you are inviting the listener to respond to. That can be receiving Jesus Christ as one's Savior, asking the Holy Spirit to sanctify entirely, asking the believer to make a commitment to Christ in one of many spiritual disciplines possible or some other way to obey the guidance of the Holy Spirit.

If using a song or hymn as support or as a backdrop to an altar call, remember always to use music and words that reinforce what you have preached about in the sermon. An altar call is not the occasion to be confusing in what you are requesting from the audience.

Many people who respond to an altar call may say yes but not know how to drink from the life-giving water of Christ. To drink, one needs to *pray through, committing to Jesus readily by faith.* A preacher should be willing and able to pay the price in praying through with seekers hungry for God.

Remember: Not only the great sermons by Billy Graham but also examples of the authenticity and direct approach of the altar calls he gave as an evangelist can readily be found on YouTube.

More Prudent Gems in Closing

If and when God gives you visible spiritual fruit from the preached Word, take the positive response with humility and grace. Consciously focus on providing the glory to Jesus even in the joys that follow preaching the Word. Do the very same even if there is no visible spiritual fruit.

The time following a good sermon as you feel emotionally and physically drained can be some of the weakest moments for a preacher, with the danger of facing a variety of temptations. *Depend strongly on God* and quickly get back to resting and walking humbly with Christ, doing justly before others, and giving all glory to His holy name. Keeping your spiritual defense shields up continuously is especially important for at least twenty hours after pouring out your soul, emotions, and physical exertion in proclaiming the Word as a prophet of God.

Remember: after the resurrection of Jesus the scene goes to the seemingly mundane event of breakfast on the seashore (John 21). Previously after the miracle of the transfiguration we see Jesus dealing with a demon-possessed boy (Matthew 17:1–20), and after the incarnation Jesus goes into the ordinary life of a child (Luke 2:41–52). I am trying to say to the speaker of God's Word that while the pinnacle moments of preaching are not necessarily always followed by anticlimactic situations, in the revelation of God's Word the preacher must be careful to keep his or her guard up in the ever-present fight against Satan.

There is no higher priority for today's pastor and preachers than the expository preaching of God's Word under the anointing of the Holy Spirit. It is the greatest need of the 21st-century church congregation and any other public spiritual gathering.

Every aspect of a preacher's life and relationships with others must be in obedience to Jesus. The quiet assurance that all is well is nothing less than the peace of God in his or her life. It is my prayer as well that you have a loving family support system that will complement the call of God on your life.

Even if you do not, God is well able to compensate, enabling and empowering you to be shameless and audacious in proclaiming His Word.

When you have faithfully done your part with robust passion, you then commit the results, the fruit, to God. Sometimes the best fruit for the preached Word may not be known to you on this side of eternity. Stand firm in the grace of God and be a strong spiritual fighter within the kingdom of God. Be the best Holiness preacher He wants you to be. The development of our lives is in His hands; therefore, let us live holy and godly lives in all the details of our existence.

Please keep the following in your mind and soul as long as you live:

The apostle Paul writes, "Be diligent to present yourself approved to God, a worker who does not need to be ashamed, rightly dividing the word of truth" (2 Timothy 2:15 NKJV).

In a devotional referring to these words written by Paul to his spiritual son and fellow preacher, Timothy, Oswald Chambers expounds well—

> *If you cannot express yourself well on each of your beliefs, work and study until you can. If you don't, other people may miss out on the blessings that come from knowing the truth. Strive to re-express the truth of God to yourself clearly and understandably, and God will use that same explanation when you share it with someone else. But you must*

be willing to go through God's winepress where the grapes crushed. You must struggle, experiment, and rehearse your words to express God's truth clearly. Then the time will come when that very expression will become God's wine of strength to someone else. But if you are not diligent and say, "I'm not going to study and struggle to express this truth in my own words; I'll just borrow my words from someone else," then the words will be of no value to you or others. Try to state to yourself what you believe to be the absolute truth of God, and you will be allowing God the opportunity to pass it on through you to someone else.

Always make it a practice to stir your own mind thoroughly to think through what you have easily believed. Your position is not really yours until you make it yours through suffering and study. (Oswald Chambers, *My Utmost for His Highest*, December 15 devotional)

By now I suspect that most readers will clearly appreciate that the shepherding and feeding of human sheep by preachers is an immense joy and great responsibility. Foremost, preaching helps to precipitate the blunt love force that sharing the gospel awakens in the inner conscience and spiritual heart of believers and also in persons outside of Christ.

Remember—it is the Holy Spirit who gives all grace via the cross of Christ, who awakens, convicts, and produces eternal fruit. Nevertheless, He has called preachers to be co-laborers with Him in sharing the precious gospel. Wow!

A great preacher once said, "There are very few joyful and happy older people *unless they know Jesus as their Lord and Savior.*" I believe it, and if you do not appreciate my statement, go and spend some top-quality time in a senior citizen home environment. Along with others, some of the most joyful and peaceful people you will see are genuine preachers who have done their best in strictly belonging to and following Jesus in and out of the pulpit. Indeed, as one grows older he or she can become increasingly less disturbed amidst even unpleasant circumstances.

Preach the Scriptures with all of God's best in you, and you will find the greatest fulfillment in your journey and in the last years of your life. Let your life find the favor of God as did the Old Testament patriarch and evangelist Noah (see Genesis 6:8, 22, in the context of the entire chapter). Like Noah of old, preach today the "everlasting ark, Jesus" with authority and without apology.

Reflect with me on an old chorus I learned in Jamaica:

> *Heaven is better than this . . .*
> *Walking those streets of shining gold . . .*
> *I love the preaching and testimonies too,*
> *But heaven is better than this.*

Hallelujah! The best is coming soon for all the blood-washed, redeemed children who are faithful to the end. Therefore, "I will hasten and not delay to obey your [our Lord and Master's] commands" (Psalm 119:60 NIV).

Jude closes with one of the most potent benedictions in Jesus's New Testament church, and I would like to reaffirm it: "Now to him who is able to protect you from stumbling and to make you stand in the presence of his glory, without blemish and with great joy, to the only God our Savior, through Jesus Christ our Lord, be glory, majesty, power, and authority before all time, now and forever. Amen" (Jude 24–25 CSB).

NOTES

1. W. Turner, E. Deibler, and J. Turner, *Jude: A Structural Commentary,* vol. 44 (Lampeter, Wales: The Edwin Mellen Press, 1996), 5.

2. Ibid., 6.

3. *The New Interpreters Bible,* vol. 12, *Hebrews to Revelation* (Nashville: Abingdon Press, 1998), 476–77.

4. Ibid., 478–79.

5. Richard Bauckham, *World Biblical Commentary,* vol. 50 (Waco, Tex.: Word Books, 1983), 4–5.

6. Ibid., 7.

7. William Barclay, *The Letters of John and Jude* (Philadelphia: Westminster Press, 1960), 197–203.

8. Bauckham, *World Biblical Commentary,* 13.

9. John J. Pilch and Bruch J. Molina, eds., *Biblical Social Values and Their Meanings: A Handbook* (Peabody, Mass.: Hendrickson Publishers, 1993), 107.

10. Turner et al., *Jude: A Structural Commentary*, 5.

11. Ibid., 6–7

12. *The New Interpreters Bible*, vol. 12, 477.

13. William W. Klein, Craig L. Bloomberg, and Robert L. Hubbard Jr., *Introduction to Biblical Interpretation* (Dallas: Word Publishing, 1993), 360.

14. *Beacon Bible Commentary*, vol. 10, *Hebrews—Revelation* (Kansas City: Beacon Hill Press of Kansas City, 1967), 424.

15. Ibid., 425.

16. Ibid., 425-26. Adapted.

17. John Wesley, Adam Clarke, Matthew Henry, et al., *One Volume New Testament Commentary* (Grand Rapids: Baker Book House, 1957), 33.

18. http://khouse.org/articles/2017/1305/

RECOMMENDATIONS for
FURTHER READING

Arthurs, Jeffrey D. *Preaching with Variety: How to Re-create the Dynamics of Biblical Genres.* Grand Rapids: Kregel Publications, 2007.

Goldsworthy, Graeme. *Preaching the Whole Bible as Christian Scripture: The Application of Biblical Theology to Expository Preaching.* Grand Rapids: William B. Eerdmans Publishing Company, 2000.

Greidanus, Sidney. *Preaching Christ from the Old Testament: A Contemporary Hermeneutical Model.* Grand Rapids: William B. Eerdmans Publishing Company, 1999.

Johnston, Graham. *Preaching to a Postmodern World: A Guide to Reaching Twenty-first Century Listeners.* Grand Rapids: Baker Books, 2001.

Mitchell, Henry. *Black Preaching: The Recovery of a Powerful Art.* Nashville: Abingdon Press, 1990.

Robinson, Haddon W. *Biblical Preaching: The Development and Delivery of Expository Messages.* Ada, Mich.: Baker Academic, 2001.

Warner, Laceye C. *Saving Women: Retrieving Evangelistic Theology and Practice.* Waco, Tex.: Baylor University Press, 2007.

Wiersbe, Warren W. *Preaching and Teaching with Imagination: The Quest for Biblical Ministry,* Grand Rapids: Baker Books, 1997.

ABOUT the AUTHOR

Rudy Morgan was born to Dr. John and Mrs. Pearl Morgan in Jamaica, West Indies, in 1958. He has been a disciple of Christ since his conversion in 1972 and has continued his faith journey by the grace of God. He was called to preach and minister the gospel in 1975.

He has been married to Ann since 1980, and they have two grown children they are very proud of: Stephanie, who is married to Jay; and Casey. His love for Jesus is paramount, and he continues to serve others in every way that God allows.

He has been an ordained elder in the Church of the Nazarene since 1984 and has an earned Ph.D. in biblical studies. He loves to preach and teach the Word of God.

Your feedback and questions are welcomed at
sluggymorgan@aol.com

Made in the USA
Middletown, DE
16 March 2025